Cool Holiday Parties

Perfect Party Planning for Kids

Karen Latchana Kenney

A Division of ABDO
ABDO
Publishing Company

visit us at www.abdopublishing.com

Published by ABDO Publishing Company, a division of ABDO, P.O. Box 398166, Minneapolis, Minnesota 55439. Copyright © 2012 by Abdo Consulting Group, Inc. International copyrights reserved in all countries. No part of this book may be reproduced in any form without written permission from the publisher. Checkerboard Library™ is a trademark and logo of ABDO Publishing Company.

Printed in the United States of America, North Mankato, Minnesota
052011
092011

 PRINTED ON RECYCLED PAPER

Interior Design and Production: Colleen Dolphin, Mighty Media, Inc.
Cover Design: Aaron DeYoe
Series Editor: Liz Salzmann
Photo Credits: Colleen Dolphin, Shutterstock

The following manufacturers/names appearing in this book are trademarks:
Aura Cacia® Peppermint Pure Essential Oil, Elmer's® 3-D Washable Glitter Paint Pens, Ferry-Morse® Seeds, Karo® Light Corn Syrup, Market Pantry® Pure Vanilla Extract, Morton® Salt, National Home Gardening Club® Seeds, Pyrex® Measuring Glass, Reynolds® Cut-Rite® Wax Paper, Scotch® Scrapbooking Tape, TruTemp® Candy Thermometer

Library of Congress Cataloging-in-Publication Data

Kenney, Karen Latchana.
  Cool holiday parties : perfect party planning for kids / Karen Latchana Kenney.
      p. cm. -- (Cool parties)
  Includes index.
  ISBN 978-1-61714-974-0
  1. Children's parties--Planning--Juvenile literature. 2. Holidays--United States--Juvenile literature. I. Title.
  GV1205.K458 2012
  793.2'1--dc22
                          2011003504

Contents

It's Holiday Party Time!

A holiday means it is time to celebrate something. On Earth Day you celebrate nature and the earth. And on Valentine's Day you celebrate love and friendship. Whatever the holiday, it can be even more fun to have a party for it! Just make the holiday your party theme. It will be a blast!

But to make this party happen, you need to plan out the **details**. Start with the basics, like the *when* and *where* of the party. Then move on to details like decorations and **menus**. Create some cool invitations and send them out. And don't forget to plan the activities! They keep the party moving at a fun pace.

Remember to plan and do as much as you can before the party starts. It takes time and hard work to be a host. But it's definitely worth it! Then all that's left for you to do is have fun!

Safety

◎ Ask for an adult's help when making food for your party.

◎ Find out where you can make crafts and play games. Do you need to protect a table surface? What should you use?

◎ Check the party room. Can anything be broken easily? Ask a parent to remove it before the party.

Permission

◎ Where in the house can you have the party? Are any rooms off-limits?

◎ How much money can you spend? Where can you shop and who will take you?

◎ Make sure guests' parents know who will be overseeing the party.

◎ Can you put up decorations? How?

◎ How long should the party last? When should guests go home?

◎ Talk about who will clean up after the party.

Party Planning Basics

Every great party has the same basic **details**. They are the *who, what, when,* and *where* of the party. Your party planning should begin with these basics. Then make lists of everything you need to buy, make, and do for the party. You should also have a list of everyone you invited. Mark whether each guest can come or not.

Who: How many friends do you want to invite? And who will they be? Try to pick friends who will get along and have fun.

What: What holiday is the party for? You'll need to explain this on the invitation.

When: Holiday parties are best on the day of the holiday. But if that won't work, pick a Saturday or a Sunday.

Where: Is the party at your house, at a park, or at a party room? Explain the details to your guests. And, don't forget to include directions!

Favors:

What to buy:

What to make:

Activities:

What to buy:

What to make:

Menu:

Decorations:

What to buy:

What to make:

Music:

Equipment:

Guests:

_____ yes/no

_____ yes/no

_____ yes/no

_____ yes/no

_____ yes/no

_____ yes/no

What's Your Theme?

What holiday do you want to celebrate? Maybe it's a holiday that you celebrate every year. Or you could **research** holidays and find one you don't know much about. Learn about the holiday's **traditions**. Are there special colors used on that holiday? What foods are usually served? Find out if it has special games, music, or dances.

Plan all the **details** around the holiday theme. From food to favors and invitations to games, the party details can relate to the holiday you are celebrating. Using a theme makes all the elements of your party go together. Check out the party themes on the next page. There are activities in this book to match each one.

New Year's Day

Each year ends on December 31st, and the new year begins on January 1st. Celebrate with party hats and loud noisemakers. Throw **confetti** and sing "Auld Lang Syne."

Valentine's Day

Show your friends and family that you love them on February 14th. Use a lot of red and pink. Decorate with hearts and cupids. Make cards for your favorite people.

St. Patrick's Day

March 17th is the day to honor everything Irish. Go to a parade and wear something green! Use **shamrocks**, **leprechauns**, and Irish flags to decorate.

Earth Day

Celebrate nature and the Earth on April 22nd. It is a great time to learn about recycling. Think of ways to reduce waste in your home.

May Day

In spring, the weather gets warmer and plants begin growing. People celebrate this time on May 1st. Flowers and maypoles are important to this holiday.

Independence Day

On July 4th, 1776, the United States **declared** independence from England. We celebrate this day with fireworks and parades. Decorate in red, white, and blue.

Halloween

When can you wear spooky costumes and get tons of treats? On October 31st! Use bats and spider webs to decorate. Orange and black are the Halloween colors.

Don't forget...

After you pick your theme, let guests know all about it. Do they need to bring something or wear special clothes? Let them know on the invitation. That way guests will show up prepared. They'll also be even more excited to party!

Tools & Supplies

Here are some of the things you'll need to do the activities in this book:

salted peanuts, chopped

juice glass

light corn syrup

vanilla extract

green food coloring

wooden stir stick

craft sticks

wax paper

butter

glass measuring cup

bowl

saucepan

baking sheet

brown sugar

salt

sweetened condensed milk

clear glycerin soap

candy thermometer

blue pencils, unsharpened

colored paper

hole punch

florist's marbles

flower seeds

scissors, deckle-edge

ribbon

florist's foam

soap molds

tissue paper, green

double-sided tape

glitter glue

glitter

card stock

scrapbook paper,
4th of July-theme

peppermint
essential oil

felt

potting soil

paintbrushes

thumbtacks

decorative gems

small flower pot

paints

wooden dowels

My Valentine Invitation

Decorative hearts make this invite so sweet!

What You Need

pink card stock
ruler
deckle-edge scissors
red and pink felt
scissors
glue
markers
glitter glue
red or pink pen

Won't You Be My Party Guest?

What: Valentine's Party!
When: February 14th
Where: 26 Central Ave, 6:00 p.m.

Bring Valentines to share!!

Valentine's Day Theme

1 Cut the card stock into rectangles. Make them 4 x 6 inches (10 x 15 cm). Cut them with deckle-edge scissors to give them a fun border.

2 Cut little hearts out of red felt. Cut slightly smaller hearts out of pink felt.

3 Glue the hearts to the card. Try gluing the smaller hearts on the bigger ones.

4 Write the name of the party at the top of the card. Think of something fun, such as "Won't You Be My Party Guest?" Write it in big letters with glitter glue.

5 Write the party **details** below the name. Use a red or pink pen. Don't forget to include anything guests need to bring.

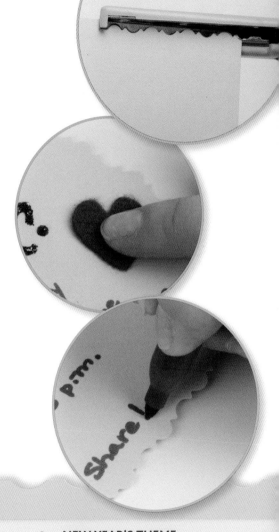

More Ideas!

EARTH DAY THEME
Make cards you can plant! **Soak** scrap paper in water. Blend it with water in a blender. Add wildflower seeds. Pour it through a strainer. Spread it in a thin layer on felt. Let it dry.

HALLOWEEN THEME
Fold a piece of orange card stock in half. Draw a pumpkin with the top of the stem at the fold. Cut it out, but leave the card stock halves connected at the top. Draw a jack-o-lantern face on it.

NEW YEAR'S THEME
Cut the year's numbers out of card stock. Then cover the numbers with glue and glitter. Glue the numbers to a colored note card.

Maypole Mini Pot

These are a May Day tradition!

What You Need

- small flower pot
- paint
- paintbrushes
- florist's foam
- scissors
- wooden dowel, 12 inches (30 cm)
- ribbon, three colors
- tape
- florist's marbles
- ruler
- paper
- markers
- glue

May Day Theme

1. Paint a flower **design** on the pot. Cut a piece of florist's foam and put it in the pot.

2. Choose two colors of ribbon. Tape one end of a ribbon to the end of the dowel. Wrap the ribbon around the dowel. Leave a space between turns of the ribbon. Tape the end to the end of the dowel. Repeat with the second ribbon. Wrap it so it fills in the space left by the first ribbon.

3. Stick the dowel in the center of the foam. Make sure it is straight. Cover the foam with marbles.

4. Cut two pieces of each color of ribbon. They should be about 18 inches (46 cm) long. Tie the ribbons to the top of the dowel. Arrange them around the pot.

5. Draw and cut out two flowers. Make them as much alike as possible. Glue one to each side of the pole.

More Ideas!

VALENTINE'S DAY THEME
Make pink and red pom-poms. Stack eight sheets of tissue paper. Make 1½-inch (4 cm) accordion folds. Tie the middle with wire. Trim the ends into points. Gently fluff out the ends.

INDEPENDENCE DAY THEME
Divide mailing labels in half. Color an American flag on the right side of each label. Wrap the labels around the tops of toothpicks. Stick the flags into the tops of cupcakes.

ST. PATRICK'S DAY THEME
Cut a bunch of **shamrock** shapes out of green paper. Decorate them with green glitter. Cut a long, green streamer. Glue the shamrocks to the streamer to make a banner.

15

Newspaper Seedling Pot

Start seedlings in biodegradable pots!

What You Need

newspaper
ruler
scissors
juice glass
tray
potting soil
seeds

Earth Day Theme

1. Make the seedling pots three to four weeks before your party. Cut sheets of newspaper into strips. They should be 3 x 22 inches (8 x 56 cm).

2. Wrap a newspaper strip around the juice glass. Let 1 inch (3 cm) of the newspaper hang below the bottom of the glass.

3. Fold the paper over the bottom of the glass. Turn the glass over and set it on the tray. Press the glass firmly against the tray. Then remove the glass. The newspaper is now a little pot.

4. Fill the pot with potting soil. Lightly press a seed into the top of the soil. Make a pot for each guest, plus a few extra. Sometimes seeds do not grow well.

5. Put the tray of seedling pots near a sunny window. Water them every day. The plants should grow more than two leaves in time for your party. Tell your guests they can plant their pots in the ground!

More Ideas!

INDEPENDENCE DAY THEME
Make flag pins. Put red, white, and blue beads onto ten safety pins. Arrange the beads to look like a flag when the pins are next to each other. Put the beaded pins on a larger safety pin.

HALLOWEEN THEME
Get a small pumpkin for each guest. Use black paint or markers to draw jack-o-lantern faces on the pumpkins. Make some happy, some scary, and some funny!

NEW YEAR'S DAY THEME
Make fun noisemakers for your guests. Put some rice, pasta, or dried beans in small plastic bottles. Use colored tape to decorate the bottles.

What's on the Menu?

A great party isn't complete without delicious snacks and cool drinks! It's best to make finger foods. They are fun to eat and easy to carry. Everyone can still mingle while they snack. To plan your party **menu**, think about a few things first.

Variety

Everyone has different tastes. Make sure you have some sweet and some salty things. Have healthy choices and **vegetarian** dishes too.

Meals

Will your party last a long time? You will need more than just snacks if it does. Think about the time of day when your party will take place. Will your guests need breakfast, lunch, or dinner? And maybe they'll want snacks too!

Amount

How many people are coming? Plan to have enough food to feed everyone.

Time

It takes time to shop for and prepare food. Pick recipes that you have time to make. Remember, there are other things you need to do before the party.

Allergies

Check with your guests to see if they have any food **allergies**. Make sure there are things those guests can eat.

Sample Party Menus

It's fun to plan your menu around your party theme. Here are some examples.

Spooky Halloween Menu

Hand-Shaped Gelatin Finger Food

Bubbly Soup in a Cauldron

Mummy-Wrapped Hot Dogs

Caramel Nut Apples*
*recipe on page 22!

Slimy Punch

Hearty St. Patrick's Day Menu

Irish Cheddar Cheese Cubes

Super Green Salad

Soda Bread and Corned Beef Sandwiches

Oatmeal Cookies

Peppermint Milk Shakes

Be Mine
Valentine's Day
Menu

Strawberry and Raspberry Fruit Cups

Cream Cheese and Strawberry Jam Roll-Ups

Heart-Shaped Pizzas

Pink Macaroons

Ruby Red Fizz

Happy Spring
May Day
Menu

Cucumber and Carrot Ribbon Salad

Couscous with Young Garden Peas

Fresh Falafel Balls

Citrus Cake

Lemon Sorbet Punch

Ask for help finding easy and delicious recipes to make.

Caramel Nut Apples

A delicious way to eat sweet, crisp apples!

What You Need

wax paper

baking sheet

measuring cups and spoons

10 apples

bowl

1 cup chopped salted peanuts

½ cup butter

saucepan

2 cups brown sugar

1 cup light corn syrup

salt

spoon

14 ounce can of sweetened condensed milk

candy thermometer

1 teaspoon vanilla extract

10 craft sticks

Halloween Theme

1. Cover the baking sheet with wax paper. Wash the apples and remove their stems. Pour the peanuts into a bowl.

2. Melt the butter in the saucepan over **medium** heat. Add the sugar, corn syrup, and a dash of salt. Cook the mixture for 10 to 12 minutes. Don't forget to stir! Keep cooking it until the mixture boils.

3. Add the sweetened condensed milk. Put the candy **thermometer** in the saucepan. Keep cooking until it is 248 degrees. Take the saucepan off the heat. Stir in the vanilla extract. This is the **caramel** sauce.

4. Push a craft stick into the top of each apple. Then dip each apple in the caramel sauce until it is covered.

5. Press the bottoms of the apples into the peanuts. Set them on the baking sheet. Put the baking sheet in the refrigerator until the caramel hardens.

New Year's Party Hat

Sparkly hats make a party!

Happy New Year!

New Year's Day Theme

1. Choose two colors of paper. Trace around the plate on each piece of paper. Cut out the two circles. Lay the circles down so they overlap by one-third. Glue them together where they overlap. Let the glue dry.

2. Write "Happy New Year!" on the top circle. Make **designs** with glitter glue and add some decorative gems. Let the glue dry.

3. Cut four pieces of silver ribbon. They should be about 16 inches (41 cm) long. Fold each ribbon in half. Tie the folded ends together in a knot. Turn the circles over. Tape the knot to the top where the circles meet.

4. Bend the sides of the circles up until they overlap by one-third. Use double-sided tape to hold the sides together where they overlap.

5. Cut two ribbons about 12 inches (30 cm) long. Tape a ribbon on each side of the hat. Tape them to the inside near the bottom. To wear your hat, tie the ribbons under your chin.

More Ideas!

ST. PATRICK'S DAY THEME
Have a pot-o-gold treasure hunt. Hide little pots filled with chocolate coins. Write clues to the hiding places. Then let your guests find the treasures!

HALLOWEEN THEME
Create a scary haunted room. Make it dark and use spider and bat decorations. Have some friends dress up and hide. They jump out and scare the guests as they walk by.

MAY DAY THEME
Make nature crowns! Make a ring of artificial ivy. Tie several ribbons around the ivy. Leave the ends long. Tie on a few artificial flowers.

Patriotic Pinwheels

Watch these fun wheels turn in the wind!

26

Independence Day Theme

1 Cut a 5¼-inch (13 cm) square out of scrapbook paper. Fold the square **diagonally**. Then fold it in half so the two side points meet. Press firmly along the folds.

2 Unfold the paper. Punch a hole in each corner on the right side of the fold line.

3 Cut on the fold lines. Stop each cut ½ inch (1 cm) from the center of the square. Then punch a hole in the center of the square.

4 Put a line of glue around the edge of the square. Sprinkle red glitter on the glue. Wait for the glue to dry and then shake off the extra glitter.

5 Bend the corners with the holes to the center of the square. Line up the holes and push a thumbtack through them. Stick the thumbtack into the side of the pencil's eraser.

More Ideas!

NEW YEAR'S DAY THEME
Make a time capsule. Decorate a tin with stickers. Put things inside that remind you of the past year. Seal it and plan to open it next New Year's Day.

VALENTINE'S DAY THEME
Make hearts out of polymer clay. Poke a hole near the top of each one. Bake them according to the directions on the clay package. Then put each heart on a ribbon to make necklaces.

EARTH DAY THEME
A used snack bag can make a cute bracelet. Fold and tie strips of the bag to make small rings. Then connect the rings to make a bracelet.

Lucky Irish Soap

These cute little soaps smell and look great!

What You Need

clear glycerin soap
glass measuring cup
green food coloring
peppermint essential oil
wooden stir stick
soap molds
green tissue paper
white ribbon

28

St. Patrick's Day Theme

1 Break the soap into pieces. Put them in the measuring cup. Microwave the soap for 20 seconds. Continue microwaving the soap for 10 seconds at a time until the soap is melted. Make sure you have permission to use the microwave oven!

2 Take the soap out of the microwave. Add 4 drops of green food coloring.

3 Then add a few drops of peppermint oil. Stir the soap well.

4 Carefully pour the soap into the molds. Wash the measuring cup right away, or the soap will stick to it.

5 Wait 45 minutes for the soap to harden. Then pop the soaps out of the molds. Wrap a few soaps in green tissue paper. Tie it with a white ribbon.

More Ideas!

EARTH DAY THEME
Make a recycled milk carton bird feeder. Cut openings on opposite sides of a cardboard carton. Punch holes below the openings. Put a stick through both holes. Add bird seed and hang it in a tree.

MAY DAY THEME
Make a May Day basket for flowers. Roll card stock into a cone. Tape the edge. Punch holes on two sides. Tie a ribbon through the holes so you can hang it up.

INDEPENDENCE DAY THEME
Make a patriotic baseball cap. Start with a plain white baseball cap. Decorate it with fabric paint or puffy paint. Try drawing red and blue stars, or a flag!

Conclusion

What made your holiday party special? Was it the pink decorations for Valentine's Day? Maybe it was the great party hats for New Year's. Whatever it was, your guests definitely had a good time. But, the party room is a mess! There's still work to do. Make sure you clean up and put everything back in order. Your parents will see what a responsible party host you are.

Did your guests bring gifts? Did you keep track of who gave you what? It's important to write it down. That will make sending thank-you cards easier. Make thank-you cards that match the party's theme. Write something **unique** and personal on each guest's card. It will make your friends feel special. Then send out the cards within a week after the party.

Hosting a party is hard work! There are so many **details** to plan and things to make. In the end, though, it all comes together to make a party to remember! Holiday parties are so much fun, but what will your next party be? Check out the other books in the *Cool Parties* series for great ideas.

Glossary

allergy – sickness caused by touching, breathing, or eating certain things.

caramel – a chewy candy made from milk, butter, and burnt sugar.

confetti – small pieces of paper that are thrown in the air during celebrations.

declare – to state publicly as a fact.

design – a decorative pattern or arrangement.

detail – a small part of something.

diagonally – from one corner of a square to the opposite corner.

leprechaun – an elf from Irish folklore.

medium – not the highest or the lowest.

menu – a list of things to choose from.

research – to find out more about something.

shamrock – a small, green plant with three leaves that is the national symbol of Ireland.

soak – to leave something in a liquid for a while.

thermometer – a tool used to measure temperature.

tradition – a custom, practice, or belief passed from one generation to the next.

unique – different, unusual, or special.

vegetarian – without any meat.

Web Sites

To learn more about cool parties, visit ABDO Publishing Company on the World Wide Web at **www.abdopublishing.com**. Web sites about cool parties are featured on our book links page. These links are routinely monitored and updated to provide the most current information available.

Index